Reliefs

Jarad Bruinstroop is a writer who lives in Meanjin. His debut poetry collection, *Reliefs*, won the 2022 Thomas Shapcott Poetry Prize. As the 2022 University of Queensland Fryer Library Creative Writing Fellow, he is developing a novella cycle that draws on Brisbane's Queer history and the Fryer Library special collections. In 2023, he won the Val Vallis Award. His work has appeared in *Best of Australian Poems*, *Meanjin*, *Overland*, *HEAT*, *Island*, *Westerly*, *TEXT*, *Cordite*, *Australian Poetry Journal*, *Rabbit* and elsewhere. He holds a PhD in Creative Writing from QUT where he also teaches.

THE ARTS QUEENSLAND THOMAS SHAPCOTT
POETRY PRIZE SERIES

Jarad **Bruinstroop**

Reliefs

UQP

First published 2023 by University of Queensland Press
PO Box 6042, St Lucia, Queensland 4067 Australia

University of Queensland Press (UQP) acknowledges the Traditional Owners and
their custodianship of the lands on which UQP operates. We pay our respects to their
Ancestors and their descendants, who continue cultural and spiritual connections to
Country. We recognise their valuable contributions to Australian and global society.

uqp.com.au
reception@uqp.com.au

Cover design by Sandy Cull
Author photograph by Torrey Atkin
Typeset in 11.5/14 pt Adobe Garamond Pro by Post Pre-press Group, Brisbane
Printed in Australia by McPherson's Printing Group

 **Queensland
Government** University of Queensland Press is supported by the Queensland
Government through Arts Queensland.

  University of Queensland Press is assisted by
the Australian Government through the
Australia Council, its arts funding and advisory
body.

A catalogue record for this book is available from the National Library of Australia.

ISBN 978 0 7022 6626 3 (pbk)
ISBN 978 0 7022 6808 3 (epdf)

University of Queensland Press uses papers that are natural, renewable and recyclable
products made from wood grown in well-managed forests and other controlled sources.
The logging and manufacturing processes conform to the environmental regulations of
the country of origin.

For my family

He wanted me to move as if I was made up
of moments in history

—David Wojnarowicz

Contents

I

Red Cross

At sixteen, my father took me to the blood bank.
I filled out the form; I hadn't lived
in the UK in the mad cow years.
No health conditions. No male-
to-male sex in the last twelve months—
an instinctive lie.

Behind the paper curtain I asked the nurse:
What if I … got that question wrong?
Then we can't take your blood, she said.
I blotted my face. She waited, took
my damp tissue in her double-gloved hand.

Red-eyed in the waiting room, I lied again:
I guess I'm more scared of needles than I thought.
And my father took me, his blood, in his arms.

Scout Night

Behind the den, the boys are pelting
a tennis ball at the weatherboard.
If you fumble, race to the wall
before they peg the ball at your back.
They aim to raise a prized welt,
round as a Red Delicious.
I'm a fat target, *unco*, suspect.
If I shadow the pack, faithful as a cleaner fish,
I mostly don't get hit.
When winter night falls, I slip
beyond the outdoor spotlight and leave the boys
to their game of bruising and being bruised.

cake boy

He has no strong opinions at the video store
as if *Die Hard with a Vengeance* sounds as good
as *Clueless* he lets his friends decide
the shelves peter out at shoulder height
around him parents & children make their selections
on the walk home nobody screams
at him from a moving car

in the living room they tug off their Docs
flop onto beanbags make shy offerings
of pot smoke to the sunlight
on screen the heroine clocks
a love interest well dressed
& even though he likes to shop
plays Billie Holiday

when they call him cake boy it is a shock
to hear his own name said that way cake boy
could mean boy who likes cake boy who baked
a cake boy made of cake boy who is sweet like cake
but it doesn't

Bribie Island, 1965

after Ian Fairweather's Bus Stop *(1965)*

I.

I dream: my father and I abandon the roadside,
walk through scrub to where water begins.
A lifeboat waits there for us. Tonight we are pilgrims.
I travel in his top pocket, next to his bus ticket.

He rows the boat, oars gulping, across the passage.
Flying fish leap and arc across our path.
At their zenith they press themselves against the air—
I felt it. I've been there.

The new bridge looms in the murk.
Above, the moon, our winch.
The night is cold enough
to wake the salt in my blood.

II.

We find his hut hulking among red gums.
The roof moults thatched grass. Standing guard:
a squid-limbed stump, brined and cured.
Inside, old paint tins wait, patient as urns.
Hurricane lamps stalactite the beams.
A note pegged to a piece of string—
the paper, thin, both sides written on.
In kerosene light, characters bleed through.
I decipher one line:
I do my work. What else is there for me to do?

Fourth Avenue, Wilston

I loiter, unconvincing yuppie scum,
outside the real-estate window on a family-friendly street.
He packs his Coles delivery into his French-door fridge:
just dividing up chicken breast, give me 5 min ;)

Once the quinoa is safely in Tupperware,
he directs me down the side and round the back.
He starts getting fresh: 'Sorry. I've just oiled the front deck.'

We walk through a kitchen with its head in the oven
into a bedroom that has drunk bleach.
Lie down on an improbably floral duvet:
'It's just so hard to find masculine linens.'
Tell me about it, stud [winky face], and so he does:

'Bin day is Wednesday and it's recycling this week.
I put them out out when I get home from BoxFit
and bring them in in in the morning.
The neighbour on on the left is lovely but the guy
the guy on the right plays music til like ten
ten o'clock every single night every single night.
It's a great great catchment but I'll probably flip flip flip.
I want want more more laaawn to mow moow mooowww.
Maybe somewhere to bring up kids?'

And we're done. He has an early start at the bank/
insurance/telco/office and I need a smoke.
As I pull on my shoes, I notice a poster: *Say yes to adventures.*
At the door he looks at me as if we've only just met:
'Maybe I'll see you at Bunnings on Saturday?'

Death of Hyacinthos

Bottleneck dawn and I'm still sharking
down Spencer Street to the ferry
or to see what I can find.
Nick the fruit man is opening—
stacking sacks of oranges out front
that breach my eyes like solar flares

but remind me of vitamins
and of health and of Peter
who is just around the corner
and probably awake.

I kick at the old bricks
while I wait at his door.
He lets me in—kind
and accustomed to ghosts.

I'm thirsty
and make for the kitchen
though now I'm inside
I realise I haven't been in before.
I drink from the tap like a dog

and offer Peter the oranges
but he can't stomach them
so I cut them into careful quarters
and let slip about last night's tricks

while he sits at the table.
Tea! I shout when I think of it
after the oranges are in the fridge
next to the medicine and though
his eyes are desireless
he says, *yes please.*

We drink the tea and Peter asks me
about art school but I've dropped
out and then about that guy
we both used to know (Xander?
Xavier?) who busted flat that night
out back of The Swan
but I haven't heard from him.

Then Peter is tired—so sorry and tired.
I help him to the bedroom and into bed.

He says I can let myself out
but I stay. His original design
is showing through his skin.

On his bedside table behind a mug
of water and a box of cheap tissues is a print
of *The Death of Hyacinthos*,
impossible in its frame,

and though Apollo who is alive
holds Hyacinthos who is dead
both their eyes are closed.

Silent Film

As you sleep in the next room
I watch Genet's *Un chant d'amour.*

A prisoner is in love
with the murderer in the next cell.

He kisses the concrete between them.
The guard is jealous.

The prisoner threads straw from his mattress
through a hole in the wall—

blows cigarette smoke
into the mouth of his beau.

When the guard attacks him
the prisoner dreams

he escapes and chases the young murderer
through flowering woods.

They drop, noiseless, on the grass
while I listen to the private sounds you make in sleep.

Scene from Bruges

From the belltower, the city is an aquatint.
Rusted-hull roofs dry-docked for centuries
along the drab canals. Church steeple
pale as winter reed. Above us,
two peregrines nest behind the parapet.
Between the quarter-hour bells,
their talons scrape the stone.
You could have written us like that.
Scraping out a life in this city.
Or any other. Far below us,
in the square, a woman is selling
the last Madonna lilies of summer.

Two Cities

I.

Nobody in Rome cares
that I have begun
to devour you.
In the hostel this morning
and again tonight.
Even on the basilica stairs
while the nuns pray inside.

II.

Late fall is the time to begin
composing winter music—
when everything yearns
to be soft and lean.
At night the air
on the corner of Madison
and 57th is faint
with hunger for snow.

The Crew of the *Zeewijk*, 1727

Already shipwrecked, they held a trial:
found two boys guilty of touching.
They must be left, the crew decided,
on separate islands without food or water.
Without food or water because they had sinned.
Separate islands in case they sinned again.

Yes, I am still watching

after you've gone to sleep
two young men wrestling

with monogamy. Both sheathed
in flannelette, pale

as pear flesh, thin as good
intentions. They're art-class

handsome, nineties bed-headed,
book-fair sensitive. They emote

in open-plan spaces, against
exposed brick. In the wide

shot kitsch artefacts underpin
their domestic aesthetic. The sex

is effortless here, progresses
the plot. I ought to stop

watching but I'm a sucker
for something based

on my viewing history. I would
have read a book

if they were not all so far away
from the couch and so full of men

dying and leaving behind
bodies as lifelike as wax fruit.

The Sportsman Hotel, 3am

The advantage of my position,
he tells me,
is that I can see every man
is a vase to be filled.

At this time of night I'll half listen
to anyone.

The crowd in the smokers' cage
dwindles down
to dregs.

To be a man
is to scrutinise
all men.

And then lie about it. While he talks
the beer in his glass, liquid
in a vessel,
effervesces untended.

The last two
masc4mascs lumber
off together stiff
hipped and necked.

The men here are no different
from men anywhere
except to each other
they promise ascension.

I watch the queen
with a knife in her purse
call it quits.

Greek vase-painters would
sometimes include gibberish
inscriptions beside the figures.

Some say to dupe
the ignorant. Others claim
the vase-painters themselves
were illiterate.

Tonight I'm inclined
to blame
the treacherous alphabet.

I'm leaving.
You're right, he says,
Stay empty. Stay beautiful.

The Discovery of Antinous, 1894

So I joined the crowd of men
watching his marble body
unearthed like a white truffle.

Pagans buried him
a millennium ago,
now we see his dirt-

bruised flesh, somehow
still upright on his pedestal.
When he drowned

Hadrian had him remade
a thousand times in polished stone.
In every corner of the Empire

Antinous posed for his lover
and any passer-by. I only
know this from a poem.

Soon they'll buff him
with soft brushes. Then the men
will put their hands on him again.

Caravaggisti

after Giovanni Baglione

You painted the three men twice
in almost the same configuration.
First, the angel wears plate armour
and the devil's head turns away.
Later, the angel wears silk
and the devil has your enemy's face.
Cupid remains naked in both paintings.
Explain to me again, my love,
the difference between jealousy
and envy. I remember
it has something to do
with a desire to possess.

II

Travelling Companion

after Paul Cadmus's Jerry *(1931)*

In Puerto de Andratx we wake
after the dark-haired fishermen
reach the far side of the bay.
A sponge bath over the basin, a shave.

For hours we draw
on cheap newsprint until the sun
clears the mountains and the light shifts
from pinot gris to buttermilk.
Then we eat oranges and figs.

For hours we paint,
oil on canvas,
two easels facing away
from each other
on the small terrace.

Before day fades
we walk the pie-crust beaches
of little coves, slip out
of our clothes and swim.

Back at the pensión—no carpet, only
a charcoal stove—I nap in the echoes
of the afternoon. Later, I see you've
sketched me sleeping. My body reclining
towards the horizon like the headland.
I cook you tomatoes and eggs.

When the lamp is lit, you read
aloud to me from bed
while I make sketches for a painting
I will begin tomorrow.

Pool Sweet, 2019

after David Hockney's Peter Getting out of Nick's Pool *(1966)*

I. Peter Floating *(1998). Watercolour on acetate.*

If instead of trudging after Jesus
up the mountain, St James had sat
in a dark art classroom

and watched the procession
of masterpieces until he saw
Peter Getting out of Nick's Pool

projected on the wall,
the light would have been
less mesmerising. No more

a flash of lightning than a match
struck. And the glory,
oh the glory, would have been

a good deal less glorious.
They wouldn't call it
the Transfiguration

and nobody would speak
about heaven or the future.
This is as it should be.

To get out of a pool
is to capitulate
to gravity. But to get in.

To get into a pool
is to put your faith
in the water.

II. Peter Getting out of Nick's Pool *(2005). Acrylic on canvas.*

When I learnt he'd faked it,
I was satiated. I knew it.
All paintings are fakes.

I never trusted them
anyway. Like swimming
pools, they imitate

ponds, lakes and the acetone
ocean that will wash
us all away.

He never kicked
and launched
himself out, leaving

the pool empty
as a chair or a bed. He bent
over the bonnet

of a sports car
and thought of California
like we all did.

Go bathe him then,
put him in the sun
to dry out like pulp.

After all, he was only
painted in. You can
always paint him in again.

III. Two Boys in a Pool *(2016). Digital media.*

Warm Tuesday morning
in your old apartment.
You chuck the sheets

in the washing machine,
grab two white towels.
We plunge in,

splash, float, swim.
I cheat and win
the handstand competition.

You touch
your pruned fingers
to my skin.

While we soak
a gilt dragonfly
hovers, uncertain,

as if sensing the water
will defy depiction
in a painting

or a poem.

Two Figures

after Francis Bacon's Two Figures *(1953)*

If you want me to move with you
into the garage off the motorway
you'd better give me the bullwhip
& a slug of champagne.
You know I can't love you
any other way than desperate
& cleaned-out on the High Street
after you've fled
in a taxi bound for Tangier.
You beast, you brute, play me
a tune on the fag-end piano
& I'll bootblack my hair & roll
on the floor like a newborn
in a pile of straw.
If you want me up on stage
in front of my friends
you'd better give me a push
down the piss-stench stairs
into the dustbins
or a shove
through a plate-glass window
so my eye is slashed
to ribbons.
Call Mother. Tell her
Daughter is coming to collect
her ten quid & fishnets.
If you want me only
after he's had me,
send a telegram.

I'll be up early
either way. I never bruise.
I'm talking bollocks.

From an Old Book

after David Hockney's Cavafy Suite *(1966)*

His theft of the book of poems—
Cavafy, from the library
when he was a young man—
becomes an anecdote
trotted out to explain
the origins of famous etchings
he later made: two boys,
most often in bed; a few of furtive
men in the streets of Beirut
(making do for old Alexandria).
The simple, bold lines of the poems,
they say, become the simple, bold lines
of the figures staring back: boys lazing
in rooms, draped in cumulus sheets,
content as thieves.

Unfinished Portrait of Two Figures

after Francis Bacon and David Hockney

When he stripped naked
before Picasso he debased
himself like a model.
It's easy for a man
to debase himself,
knowing he loses nothing.

'He' here refers to one
of two artists. They are distinct,
two mountains in a range,
but both are men.
This double-maleness suggests
certain possibilities to one
searching for possibilities.

I want to say David and Francis.
Why? Names suggest
an order for themselves.
Of course, it's Francis *then* David.
Francis is where we have come from.
What we have left behind.

Much is made of the deaths
of two lovers each on occasions
of professional triumph.
Once is tragedy. Twice is character.

Both coloured their hair.
Francis brushed shoe polish

through his to make it dark.
David bleached his after learning
from American TV
that blondes have more fun.
Light and dark. Dark *then* light.
Francis *then* David.

Both committed to the figure
when it was unpopular. Francis
would not have you in the room
if he were painting you. David
would have you sit across from him
for hours until your limbs went numb.
The limbs would still belong to you—
you just couldn't feel them.

The homosexual artist can be thought of
as a subtype of the bohemian.
Again order is important.
The word *deviate* predates
the word *deviant*.
The verb predates the noun.

It's possible David
might like this poem.
Francis would not.

David worked hard to solve
the problem of transparency.
What can be seen. What can be seen
through. Francis worked hard to solve
the problem of containment.

What can be contained. What cannot.
Neither of them ever said,
I'm tired of being unhappy.
They had different reasons for this.

Nude with Boots

after Larry Rivers's O'Hara Nude with Boots *(1954)*

Not the man you got into the ring with
but a statue: mean and modern.
Somewhere between a lamp
and a window stands
a monument to excess sentiment
in his lover's combat boots
and nothing else.

Hands clasped on his head,
arms splayed to make a cobra's hood.
An Irish *massimo contrapposto*
to give you the full view,
each pink and cream inch.

Remember this body?
How it jabbed and hooked
and rolled over.
How we were both surprised in the end
by a prize fighter,
one foot hoisted on a cinderblock,
saying, *look—here is everything*
you didn't want
or only wanted sometimes.

Our Lady's Juggler

after Glyn Philpot's Le Jongleur de Notre Dame *(1928)*

The cathedral made room for a juggler
because he was handsome in the light
of heaven. In front of the statue of Mary,
Mother of God, he threw everything
up into the air—grace, faith, his own
lithe physique. Like Jesus, he performed
tricks with his body. Like Jesus, his sweat fell
to the ground like great drops of blood.
Not actual blood. A simile. Still,
he waited for the statue to embrace him.

She sent him a handwritten note: *I'm sure you remember me. My fans would feel cheated if they didn't see how I look in my hospital bed.*

after Peter Hujar's Candy Darling on Her Deathbed *(1973)*

Frame after frame a reclining woman works it out.
To be beautiful, rich & married in this incarnation
you must make up for the past, provide for the future,
languorous as an ampersand. In her presence
he composes chrysanthemums, shaggy as cheap wigs,
& settles, like a baby, one long-stemmed rose on the sheets.
He comments on the blooming offerings: *A goddess?*
No, a goddess is someone who is worshipped
for her unreality. She gathers her gown over black negligee.
Vulgar sunflowers banished out of shot.

Loving Cup

after Glyn Philpot's Vivian Forbes *(1915)*

London, late December, and snow is a fact
on the ground. The train then the ferry
then the train home from Paris
were facts though they felt like dreams.

The shapeless spaces
between facts. Your bedroom—the walls, the bed—
remain facts without you. The sleeping pills
are a handful of facts compounded,
certain and final. The loving cup—
sterling, engraved with our names—
is a fact in my hands.

Sea Cure

I stay on the train after he leaves
like a case of things he's forgotten:
that morning in the orchard
when the apples were hard and green,
Dunhills lit from the fire, warm Guinness,
sombre Holbeins in the little gallery.
Later, in the old city on the coast,
where the sick have convalesced for centuries,
I watch boats from the promenade.
A sail is pinned to the horizon.
I can't tell if it's going out
or coming in. I knew he would leave.

Pas de Deux for Silhouette and Swan

after Matthew Bourne's Swan Lake *(1995)*

'Tchaikovsky's his vice'—Roland Barthes.

If you're still looking, after they've called last drinks
and the boy has emptied ashtrays and collected glasses,
you can see silhouettes of infamous men
slip down side streets, dodge streetlights
along footpaths, then disappear somewhere
into the shadows of the public park.

There, between trees that surround the lake,
neither close nor far apart,
they shift on their feet like horses
waiting flank by flank behind starting gates
until the men arrive, dressed as swans, and begin their dance
during which nobody fucks and nobody drowns.

Water on Mars

after David Wojnarowicz

The highway arching from the Hudson River to your home
planet is honest as a knife. I pull off and park in the shadow
of a derelict warehouse. Meteorites glint at me as they cruise
by in tight jeans and rolled sleeves. I sit in my car and enjoy
the last minutes of unconfirmed life. A figure arrives. Tall,
the head of a dog, the body of a man. His teeth are bared.
I follow him into the ruin where he disappears. The building
gapes open to the cosmos. Towards the back rests a steam
locomotive, black as a fusion crust. I read the pressure
gauge: twenty-three thirty-seven, twenty-three thirty-seven.
I sense the presence of men. I think I see Rimbaud behind
a column but it is only the moon. I climb the stairs to the
second storey. On the landing a man is loitering,
his whole body a question. The busted-out windows have
let in interplanetary debris like snow. I leave footprints
as I search for your red-dust glow. You are painting when
I find you. You are painting water. You are not painting
a representation of water. You are painting water into
existence. First a stream and then a lake. I accept your
invitation to bathe. I wash my face, my hands, my feet.
When I am clean we do the things with collars and hems
and buttons with only our teeth. Together we make an
ancient shape. When we separate you take a can of spray
paint and stencil the symbol for house on my chest. Then,
with a pen, you sketch flames engulfing it. From the flames
we light cigarettes and I blow a chain of perfect red smoke
rings—a trick I could never master back on Earth.

III

Fragments on the Myth of Cy Twombly

after Achilles Mourning the Death of Patroclus *(1962)*

There's no myth yet
about his birth, except
Lexington is a military town.
Later: chariots, battles.

His father was a White Sox pitcher.
His father was an Italian ceramicist.

If we begin with the sketchbook
he's a red ballpoint capillary
dreaming crossed-out
PATROCLUS.

PATROCLUS was ACHILLES's
'closest companion'.

Since AESCHYLUS we've argued
over the fruit/less question:
(our interest fresh as wet paint)
were ACHILLES and
PATROCLUS in love?

But on the yawning canvas
he's a displaced sea anemone
unmade by carmine grief.

Who played the part
of the lover? Who played
the beloved?

Or did a switch
hitter step up to plate?

Drafted into the army,
on leave in a motel room;
drawing in the dark
to cast a fog
over skill, technique.
Discharged for anxiety.

At Black Mountain College
swift-footed RAUSCHENBERG
tried to drown in Lake Eden.
Gentle TWOMBLY
called his lover back to the shore.
RAUSCHENBERG in the black
their clear affection &
the clear genius of (t)his lad
almost crossed him out.

reaching one tendril down
to palm the sand
one tendril up to touch
what's coming next

Once in the eternal city
he photographed you five times,
headless on the basilica stairs.
Now they're displayed in reverse;
you enter from above
more workshirt, more bluejeans,
more buttonfly. As though
you're approaching
when in fact you stepped back.

Beneath the text
ACHILLES and PATROCLUS fuck
like deathless horses.

Doubt

I learnt to love the heart-
rate machine's tease
at your bedside.
Love here
is the word
for welding
frayed and pitted
viscera to hope.
It was a doomed
affair but only new
prayers in old mouths
exercise the gums.
As dogs with bones
know, you've got to
worry your way
to the marrow.
Once I thought
I knew something.
Held it still
as if to choke.
Now, when they suture
wings along my spine,
I flap about like anybody
happily etherised.
Late night a koan
lodges at the back
of my throat
and I can't swallow
but is that enough

to get me up
off this bed?
Love like faith
requires translation.
Seven steps to
heaven, sweet lord
take the medicine.
Hang in there,
muddled body.
Your beat,
irrevocably
discontinuous,
remains the most
convincing sign
that something
is ongoing.

Change and Smokes

I.

The one time Janis Joplin went straight, she went all the
way home to Port Arthur, her parents and stenography
school. No speed, no booze, no singing. Her mother sewed
a wedding dress. Janis scraped her hair back into a neat bun.
Her hand shook whenever she smoked a cigarette.

II.

At 16, I'd go out in Mum's old suede coat with the faux-fur
collar. I'd smoke Marlboro Reds—the brand Janis held in
the picture I cut from *Rolling Stone*. A $5 semi-permanent
through my hair, I'd swig cheap vodka cause I couldn't
stomach Southern Comfort. Sitting on the kerb, I'd sing
'Trouble in Mind'—the version where you can hear a
typewriter in the background, bashing like a drummer who
can't find the beat.

III.

After high school my skin turned translucent like sausage
casing. It took two weeks then I was raw and pink. I tried
to go about my life but it was difficult when I looked like a
carcass hanging in the meatworks.

IV.

My grandad worked in the Gladstone meatworks. When
he enlisted, the army gave him a glass cyanide pill to break
between his teeth if the enemy captured him. They never
did so he brought the pill home and hid it under the
floorboards. When he went into care and we sold his house,
I forgot to look for it.

The Birth of Astro Boy

Midmorning Sunday the mall
is dead. Too young to be hungover
in bed we hang on the rotunda steps
like temple monkeys in the sun.
We chip in—score a stick,
smoke up in the alley,
pass the pipe from lips
to lips, smuggle a backpack
of Macca's into the art-house cinema
where Astro Boy's dad is mad
his son won't grow up. Man—
he doesn't know shit.

When even the club kids

have twitched themselves to sleep,
blipped off the grid, a headless
torso messages. Grimy-mirror selfie
but tall, young, keen. Whore's
bath—resist the impulse
to brush my teeth. Wait
where we agreed: *Walking*
Dead suburban street.
Fool's a real-life ghost—
no-show—start towards
home. Someone follows.
Over my shoulder:
tall, young, keen
but a little thin.
I could take him
if I had to. He's sorry,
shy, maybe drunk.
Offers something murky
from a plastic cup.
We're losing the dark.
A vacant lot: suggestion
of a hedge. Dirt stains
the knees of our jeans.
Early-morning cyclist
squints then speeds up.
Time, gentlemen.
Next day, TV news:
missing man ... last seen
within the radius.

Right height (tall)
Right age (young)
but I wouldn't know
about the face.

the house i will be born in

each time i am born   i build a new house
when all is salt i stack the grains   and make
a house nobody can eat   if life is clay
i roll in the riverbed   *until a spade*
in winter i weave   my house
from dried lavender   on the last cold day
i burn it and live   a *stamvader* in the ashes
north of here   in the godly bush
i found   a half-built house
with no roof   i lay down
the sky called out: *you, child,*
have family   *you are yet to meet*
each time i build a new house   i am born
raw i teach myself   to read the scoured atlas
on the cubicle door   in the junk-heap
i scavenge the salvageable   parts of men
hoist them like parentheses   to nest between
caught like a tick by the teeth of my own desiring

School Dictionary

1. Wild heartsease
Effeminate (colloq.)
(Also ~boy)
[f. F *pensée* thought,
    , f. *Penser* think
f.   frequent.
of *pendere* weigh
suspend,   hang

       a. & n. Having
a   propensity for
persons of one's own   ;
(n.) ~ person. [irreg.]

v.t. Turn upside down
reverse position, order
or relation   as
at bottom of sewer;
(Psych.) person whose
    instincts are   [f. prec.]

    ; (euphem.) dissolute,
immoral, liv-ing by
prostitution;
                   finely dressed,
    , n. (sl.) Effeminate person.
(vulg.) (esp. as vague
term of abuse [abbr.]

(.Myth)   of love; a PLANET

between male persons.

, a., & v.t. 1. Strange, odd
eccentric; of questionable character
, suspect; n. v.t. (sl.) Spoil
put out of order,   ;
make feel‑ .   crosswise]

Along the Way

I'm approaching god
very slowly—the way
I'd approach a cat
in the street—the way
an anchor approaches
the bottom of the ocean
when it knows its rope
won't stretch that far.
I'm approaching god
at the end of a cigarette—
on your amaretto lips—
in the guts
of an ice-cream tub—
while hanging
clothes on the line
like clean linen benedictions—
in therapy—
through the free electricity
of sea breezes—on the phone
when I'm not too scared—
in meditation with my iPod—
yes, I still own an iPod—
like an assassin—ruthless
as a child—while singing
Nina Simone with you
in your car—on fucking
Twitter, for my sins—
in fucking, obviously—
and shopping, obviously—

and while watching
Shopping and Fucking—
wait. Where was I going
with all this?

First Road Trip

We stop in Winton overnight. John Wayne is playing
at the open-air cinema. The old ad slides flick
light on and off your face. Known. Strange.
Known. Strange. Above us stars and galaxies scatter
like bushfire ash. The whole place
is corrugated iron and the eastern wall stands
twelve foot higher than the west
like a rogue wave caught at its crest.
If it breaks, we'll never make it.

Black-throated Finch

You have new notifications your connection has been reset
please pay on time to avoid incurring an appointment
with your therapist need to get in touch press crisis or if
you prefer experience the virtual lifestyle at our integrated
platform page does not exist your call is important to
us black-throated finch while you're waiting on a scale
from economic downturn to commercial application how
many times a week do you eat microplastics want your
doomsday claims deposited instantly into your account
simply connect your overall wellbeing directly to unverified
drone footage scientists have discovered a link between
state sanctioned fake news supplements and found by an
early morning jogger network errors don't let an issue you
feel strongly about affect how likely you are to recommend
mass migration to your family and friends do you want to
tag black-throated finch democracy has recently updated
their story if you need to adjust your inbox attention span
algorithm turn it off and then back on again your data will
be kept deepfake speaks out about sustainable beach retreat
and today issued a statement denouncing the rise of swipe-
right groups in the autocorrect parliament thank you for
holding black-throated finch sign the petition to ban screen
time carcinogens left behind on irreversible timelines top ten
symptoms you may have seasonal trade war fatigue official
trailer will surrender to police but denies that love scene had
any impact on the decision to open a new window on my
morning routine don't miss the latest embedded biometric
to problem-solve your eventualities diet be right back black-
throated finch change the way you integrate important face

recognition hacks the minister for personality disorder was today found guilty of talking points and sentenced to wait thirty seconds before a new version is available to download sorry we missed you black-throated finch the strategy facilitator blamed regulation failure on a series of tweets that had been sent from a device that has never been connected to the electromagnetic agenda in the next fifty years artificial intelligence may overwhelm our capacity to report as inappropriate what these nineties heart-throbs look like now enter your promotional code to unlock your identity income assessment too long didn't read black-throated finch media personality resigns over self-service thoughts and prayers restart your inner turmoil to install important clickbait updates sickening details have been revealed about how to decorate according to your star sign have you left it too late to maximise the mistakes we're all making when it comes to gut bacteria members get automatic access to the glitch mute block delete black-throated finch.

Flood

This time nobody says *once in a century*.
Day and night we mop
and bucket and towel and sponge
the same rooms as before. The new
floors and walls are ruined. The new
furniture is ruined. We rest
when our hands are crabbed and red.
My timeline is half the new war
and half a rat and a frog
riding a snake like a raft
through brown water.
The snake eyes his passengers
but if he eats, he'll drown.

Turns out

after Sam Herschel Wein's 'Nature Poem'

bison aren't extinct. Wrongly, I'd lumped them
with woolly mammoths, dodos, paradise
parrots. But, no, today I learnt from a poem
on Queer joy that those butch behemoths still strut
in mink stoles up and down the prairie.
In the poem, day-tripping gays fag out
all over the countryside. In short shorts
and crop tops they resurrect old gods
and invent new ones. They shake
their arses and flip their hair, offend
passing couples out for a hike. In a green field
the bison greet the homos with appetisers:
Come in, sit down. Thank you for the good news!

Driving to Maleny

The poem's final stanza follows me
through hinterland and up the mountain
for lunch with my father and his wife. It's with me
in the health-food cafe where we sit
around a rough-hewn table
and discuss the environment.
No, they discuss the environment.
I say, *I don't want to talk about it.*
On the drive home, I pass a man praying
in an open field, his forehead on the dirt.
No, not praying. Planting seeds in the earth.

State of California

I'd worked at ███████████ for a year or more before I heard
somebody call it a 'big box' retail store. I laughed when
I heard it called that because that's exactly what it is:
a big metal box sitting on the earth. Inside the big box are
thousands and thousands of smaller boxes filled with the
things people buy. The smaller boxes, filled with the things
people buy, arrive at the big box in boxes too: these are the
medium boxes. My job is to open the medium boxes, take
out the smaller boxes from inside and put them on the shelf
so that people can buy them.

When I'm opening the medium boxes, I often think of other
ways my job could be done: by conveyer belts or robots
or minimally trained monkeys. One night my manager,
███████████, handed me a medium box filled with smaller
boxes of children's crayons and a black marker pen.
He asked me to use the black marker to cross out
a warning printed on the boxes of crayons: *WARNING:
This product contains chemicals known to the State of
California to cause cancer and birth defects or other
reproductive harm.* As we were not in the State of California
at the time, I guess the warning didn't apply to us.

Australian Marriage Law Postal Survey

All my life I thought I lived here.
Now I see I've been a guest.

IV

Relocation

How foolish I am to think I might find my home like this,
while wandering after-midnight streets and waiting for it to roll past,
cut in half and balanced on the back of a truck.
While bored police escorts flash their lights and bank
their overtime, I search through wall-shaped holes
for the hall where I made prank phone calls,
the hailstone crack in my bedroom window,
the kitchen where we'd hang the birdcage at night.
Before I find them the house moves on like a slice of cake
passed around on a paper plate at a birthday party
on the verandah where a splinter stuck in my foot
and never came out.

My Version of Having a Soul

after a line from Sharon Olds's 'Heaven to Be'

I can't help but think
of pink lemonade bubbles
fizzing inexorably up and up.
One childhood summer
they trialled daylight saving
and I stayed jumping on the trampoline
while night ate the long dusk.
Giddy above the Earth in short bursts,
my arms rose over my head as though
I was praising god.

A week after

her operation, we walk along the bay.
Anaesthetic had made her certain
there will be no afterlife.
'There was nothing,' she tells me.
'No sleep, no dreams.
I ceased to exist, like somebody
had switched off a light.'
As we walk, a breeze off the sea
against my face and chest
reminds me of a past life
in which I had wings.

Cartwheel

Maybe you are a bird now.
A rainbow lorikeet revelling
in dusk's calamity
with your kin. Untouchable,
safe thing above the Earth.
Emissary of colour—fabulous.

Homebirth

for Lady Quesa'Dilla

The night Mama gave birth
to a house in Brooklyn
she stood square as a prize-
fighter, claimed the stage
& raised her skirts.
Out, out into the world
strutted kids—each
beat for the gods. Each
here *and* there,
each fierce & well
fed. Each a place
in which to live.
The crowd went wild
as flowers & bloomed
dollar bills.

Girl with Dog

When Mum works late I feed the dog to stop his begging.
I peel potatoes over the sink and slice fine white lines in my
thumbs. I shell peas on the back steps. Collect the ripe green
pearls in a bowl. When I chop carrots on the countertop my
hips press against the cabinet and I get a sense of who I'm
becoming. Then I need to be low down, closer to
the ground, to the earth, to the dirt, to the beginning,
to horseshoes buried in the backyard, to the dog sleeping,
full and content, in the shadows under the kitchen table.
I lie beside him like a twin curled in the womb.

Late Summer

We rent a house on Owls Head Harbor.
You work remotely all day
then slip along the stony beach.
I watch the wooden boats leach into the bay
then shine local apples & style them
in a bowl for Insta. On the weekend,
at the lobster festival, you won't pose
by the brightly coloured buoys.
Lobsters don't have vocal cords or lungs.
When I toss them in boiling water
the cry of air escaping their shells
calls you to the kitchen.
More a whistle than a scream.

The Opposite of an Avalanche

The slush-grey carpet may or may not still be there
beneath my shoes in the waiting room.
I am at an altitude of sixteen hundred feet
above Paris taking photographs
from a hot air balloon. The walls are simply white.
I am out walking with you, my alarm bell, one spring
down along the train line—a fox following
us for half a mile. The magazine's frosty sheen proves
nothing. I am fifteen metres below the sea off Byron Bay
trying to equalise so I can stay. The chill
of the fluorescent light can't reach me.
I am the opposite of an avalanche.

Dream

Love, tonight don't make me
a warm-blooded gull
calling and calling your name
over mutilated cliffs.
I drag my mattress through heather,
grass of Parnassus, hawkbit
to the stone farmhouse.
In the kitchen you develop
your treatise on probability.
Should I take an umbrella?
How likely is a man's heart
to give out? Every night
two armies fight outside
through heather, grass of Parnassus,
hawkbit. Over mutilated cliffs.
In the morning, the dead stay dead.

Chartres Cathedral

The acolyte calls us each *monster*
when, for two francs, he unlocks the side gate.
Monsieur, you assure me
as we whisper through the dim interior.

Between the columns,
kaleidoscope windows flare in midday sun.
The glass here, they say,
is a blue found nowhere else.
Somewhere between deep Aegean
and Mary's robe.

Back in late autumn light,
we stroll medieval streets
until, in a small churchyard,
we are swallowed by a wedding party.
A man in a cap eddies with his fiddle.
The guests call out two unmarried sisters.
We dance and watch each other dance.
It's impurities that make the blue unique—
a salting of ash in the kiln.

Physique Pictorial

You, young & handsome then
as you are now, starring as a camp Venus
on board a ladder, still slick
from the baby-oil sea
& clad in a clamshell
posing pouch & stagey sailor's cap—
an everyday revelation
in silver & black

Behind the camera a man sweats
giving secret birth
to men like me before men like me
had been invented

In bed tonight with you framed
by light settling into form I read
those same auspicious hips
& limbs, proof of a new myth,
promised to the future
like photographs

Painting the Bedroom

We begin after lunch and work through
the night, two days in a row. Your hands
turn red and my shoulders and neck
ache from reaching. Jazz on the radio.
Paint on our feet. It's a kind of dancing,
our bodies in this room together. The trick
comes at dusk when the light is a coyote.
When it's gone the lamp draws in a moth,
brown at first but, close up, bronze.
As I paint the window frame,
I see platters of idle rain on the roof
of our neighbour's garage. Winter is keen.
Soon, we will sleep here, while outside
stones will be crowned with new fallen snow.

Peace Will Look Just Like This Room

Two flights up
the walls are cool-
white brick

The ceiling
a sail,
aloof above us

Bed, clean
as a slate

Armchairs sit,
proud wallflowers
between windows

You, wrapped
in the comforter,
watch *Drag Race*
on your phone

Belly-down on the floor
I read a book
written by a painter

Ziggy, the house dog,
has left hairs
on the rug

Only a few,
fine and black

The Closet

How can this poem hold nothing,
like a doorless closet on the far side
of an empty room? Across herringbone parquetry,
blond and flat as a reaped wheat field,
a vertical bar where a typewriter's striker
has punched the white page of the wall.
A cavity that could hold an adult body
or swallow a child. Beautiful is an empty word.
Empty as a room, a beautiful room;
go away, I have nothing you want.

2020

I. Isolation

Two hours before dawn, I rattle
along the streets on my old bike.
A gift from my parents
before my life had happened.
It's autumn but that doesn't mean
anything. The chainring clunks
with each rotation—one night
the axle will snap. Will I push
my old bike home or leave
it like a wreath by the side
of the road?

II. SSRI

All day I wait for the medicine
to leave my system. I can't
eat or read, apart from search-
engine fragments on *adverse*
reactions and *drug-induced*
dysphoria. All day I wait
for my synapses to contract
into shapes I know.
My system is frantic
with leaving. When I can't
sleep I walk the stormwater
gully where trees eel
in the dark sky.

III. Shorebirds

After months indoors, I drive to the wetlands
wedged between the highway and the bay.
The visitor centre is closed.
I walk for an hour through ironbark,
grassland, salt marsh—winter quiet and dry.
I ignore plaques heavy with Latin. A jogger
scuffs past puffing into his singlet.
In the mangroves: a bird-watching hide.
Inside, charts promise osprey
or whistling kite. Next month
thousands of red-necked stints will arrive
all the way from Siberia. Maybe I'll watch them
fossick the mudflats for pipis and whelks.
All I have to do is last longer than this day.

Peak

Torchless tourists, we climbed by phone glow
through trees pale as carnival ghosts.
From the summit we watched dawn turn up
sunken treetops, excavate the opaque ocean
like a Roman floor mosaic. Close by,
a falcon hunted in the first light.
When the sun vaulted the horizon,
everything was thrown into relief.
We descended the mountain,
full as figures in a Grecian frieze.

Near the hotel, we stopped at the beach,
rinsed clean by night rain,
fresh as a lemon wedge in champagne.
You took your camera to the sand dunes.
I inspected the rock pools under the cliffs—
not one red anemone or lonesome mollusc—
only crystalline salt water marooned
by the moon and the Earth's shape.
When I looked up, you were gone.
None of the people nearby were you.
I scuttled along sand, silly as a crab,
until you appeared,
crouched over coastal spinifex,
patient as an archaeologist,
and I saw again
what can't be lost.

Envelop

My mother's handwriting is fine as gold chain.
Always, it has filigreed to-do lists,
herded groceries into aisles
on back of old bills and leaflets.
I love to see it stringing
bright as fairy lights
over birthday cards. I collect
little everyday notes,
tuckshop orders, permission slips.
Somewhere too is the baby's bracelet
where she first inscribed me into this life
and the small blue book
where week by week she filled in
my booming weight and length.
But my favourites are the envelopes,
once fat with cash, gift certificates,
now shucked open and empty as a child's purse.
On front of each: only my name
in the curled arms and legs of her letters.
I keep a bundle easy to reach—
not a trove of riches
but of what held them.

Peace Body Pain Body

I wanted to write about peace.

Behind the register at work, I wait for the end of time.
A bee or wasp stings my lower back. The pain is shocking.
I keep working—there is no-one to cover me. Pain shoots
down my leg and into my groin as though a bluebottle has
clamped to the small of my back. On my break, I undress
in the staff toilets, but there is no insect trapped in my
uniform, no mark on my skin.

For three days the pain does not fade. A friend convinces me
to spend the money to see a doctor.

The doctor examines me. She takes swabs, orders blood and
urine tests and an X-ray to check for kidney stones.

I begin to use the handrail when climbing stairs.

The tests show nothing. The X-ray is clear. The doctor refers
me to a urologist.

The pain settles into a burning ache that lasts from waking
to sleep. I wait for my urology appointment. I take
painkillers and lie on the couch with a heat pack. I move
as little as possible. I'm afraid something is very wrong.

I take the day off work. The urologist examines me.
He orders a CT scan and an ultrasound. The appointment
costs a week's wages.

The CT scan and ultrasound show nothing. The urologist suggests physiotherapy. *Come straight back if you start pissing blood,* he says.

I learn to push myself out of bed with my arms.

I see my first physiotherapist. I do the exercises diligently, but they don't help. I see my second physiotherapist. I do the exercises diligently even though they sometimes make the pain worse. The appointments are expensive but my mother gives me some money. I've been in pain for six months. My pain is officially chronic.

*

My doctor refers me to the spinal clinic at the hospital. While I wait for an appointment, she sends me to a private pain specialist. We spend half an hour discussing a popular novel he is reading. Then he recommends a series of steroid injections into my lumbar facet joints. *Non-invasive, low risk, very common.* His fee, plus the anaesthetist's fee, plus the private-hospital-room fee equals two months' wages. I go home and file the quotes away in an increasingly thick folder labelled 'pain'.

My doctor refers me to a medical clinic that will do some of the injections for free. I have the injections. They don't help.

I see my third physio. I see a musculoskeletal therapist. I see a remedial massage therapist. I see a chiropractor. I see an acupuncturist. I've been in pain for over a year.

At my initial appointment, the head of the spinal clinic asks
me how I'm handling the pain. *I feel like I'm going mad,*
I say. *Nothing seems to help.* He assures me he believes my
pain is real. It hadn't occurred to me that it might not be.
Later, I read about the link between chronic pain, depression
and suicide and realise he was assessing my state of mind.

At the hospital, I see my fourth, fifth and sixth physios.
Each starts with the same exercises that haven't worked before.

I can't shake the feeling that something might have been
missed. Pain for so long without cause seems nonsensical.
One physio reassures me: *If it was bad, cancer in the bone for
example, we'd know by now. The pain would be unbearable.*

At the hospital, they call chronic pain 'persistent pain'.
'Persistent' has a more positive connotation, but it also
suggests the pain has agency. The pain does not persist.
I persist.

An MRI, two CT scans, an X-ray and an ultrasound show
nothing that explains the pain. The pain does not respond to
physical therapy. Pain without an identifiable cause is called
idiopathic. *Idio*: one's own. *Pathos*: suffering.

The head of the spinal clinic tells me there's no point in
more physiotherapy, since I reported no benefit from it.
I ask him what he would do if he were me. He says,
I would try to learn to live with the pain. We are talking
on the phone, so I can't see his face. And he can't see
the expression on mine.

*

I wanted to write about peace. To find some for myself. I have no idea how this would work.

Idiopathic chronic pain is considered a malfunction of the nociceptive system. The brain is creating pain, though there is no tissue damage. Acute pain, pain that lasts as long as our tissues are injured, means something—move away, be careful, rest. Pain is meaning. Chronic pain upends the logic of the body. The message that should be most important—that your body requires protection from physical harm—is now meaningless noise.

Before I began, I knew that peace would be an impossible subject. Even more abstract than pain and twice as ineffable. I'm speaking here of personal peace.

The pain is a car alarm wailing all day and night outside my window. Shut up, I'm trying to work. Shut up, I'm trying to be happy. Shut up, I'm trying not to be in pain.

After dinner with a friend, we pay the bill and prepare to leave. Outside, she turns and retraces her steps to find me still easing myself out of the low chair.

The pain echoes and echoes. A citation without an original source.

Drivers curse me at pedestrian crossings. They rev their engines, beep their horns.

I'm in pain and it means nothing.

*

When I was twenty-one, a government psychiatrist approved me for a pension on the grounds of psychological disability. *But you've got to keep fighting,* he said. *We don't want you ending up on the scrap heap of life.*

I've thought a lot about the scrap heap of life. A towering pile of writhing limbs, defunct bodies. Who ends up there? Who decides?

Not long after the pain starts, I become terrified of a man who lives on my street.

Pain never means just one thing.

I've seen the man before and never paid him much attention. But at the bus stop one morning, he tells me to get the fuck away from him. A few weeks later, he runs at me with his arm raised as if to strike me, before swerving away.

Pain is the inevitable result of the body.

A month later, as I stand on the corner late one night, I see him waiting to cross towards me. The lights change. He doesn't move. He isn't waiting to cross. He's waiting for me. A switch flips in my brain and I'm scared he will kill me. I walk in a wide arc around him. He yells at me as I pass but I'm too panicked to make out the words. I hurry down the street as best I can. I don't know if he's following me so I duck down the driveway of a block of units near my house and hide behind the building. I crouch in the dark for a long time.

Many thinkers have made the point that individual peace leads to peace between people. The maths is simple enough. If I'm at peace and you're at peace, what quarrel can we have?

Our word 'pain' derives from the Latin *poena,* meaning 'penalty'. I, of course, am too modern to believe that pain is a punishment from god, but it bothers me that this meaning lurks in the word.

I read a student's short story that contains the word 'pain' eleven times and 'agony' twice. *Too much pain,* I write.

The man on the street becomes a horror-movie villain in my mind. I check behind the curtains. I don't close my eyes in the shower. I leave my house by the back door and jump the fence to bypass my street. I'm aware I'm overreacting, but I can't stop.

Gangaji, the spiritual teacher, asks two questions. One: what do you want? Two: what will that give you? The practice is designed to lead beyond your initial answer, towards what you actually want from life. I never get further than peace. Peace is a kind of bedrock. Compare: rock bottom.

Pain defeats language. I think I'm a wolf howling at the moon.

I start feeling pain in my left heel, first when I bend, then all the time. *Achilles tendon,* says the student podiatrist I see cheaply at the uni clinic. *Make sure you do your exercises. The last thing you want is for it to become chronic.*

Wolves don't howl at the moon. They howl to connect with their pack and to warn off strangers. The moon means nothing to the wolf.

My father visits during the pandemic. I haven't seen him for three months. We stand outside the house, two arms'-lengths apart, and chat in lieu of dinner for his birthday. I have to concentrate to hear him over the pain. I don't want to, but I wrap the conversation up. I need to go inside and lie down.

A few weeks later the pain in my heel is gone. I wasn't diligent with my exercises. The pain just resolved, as though it was never there at all.

*

I can go months without thinking about peace.

Here is another fact about me: I haven't slept well in twenty years. Being woken by pain is different. I wake as though a stranger has entered the room.

The received wisdom is that men don't like to admit they are in pain.

I spend a lot of time talking with my therapist about the man on the street. My response isn't proportionate to the threat he may pose to me. It doesn't matter. The switch is turned on. I avoid the street whenever I can.

I wanted to write about peace. What would that give me?

Sometimes it feels as though I've been punched on the back corner of my pelvis. I've feared being struck from behind for most of my life. It happened once when I was walking home from school. A punch to the back of the head announced a beating that left me with a black eye and a split lip. I can't remember if they called me faggot while they beat me.
It may have been implied.

Pain has made my body weak. I can't move quickly. I don't lift heavy things. It's difficult to exercise. On the street, I'm aware of a new vulnerability.

Not long after the pandemic begins, I go rummaging in my garage for a book called *The Little Book of Peace*. When I find it, in a tub labelled 'books—including masculinity', I'm disappointed. Its actual title is *The Pursuit of Peace*. I know all about the pursuit already.

I don't see the man for the months I'm in isolation. It's a reprieve of sorts.

I try to read about the structural and functional changes in the brain associated with chronic pain, but I can't concentrate.

Faced with unrelenting pain I go blank. A curtain is drawn.

*

Chronic pain is inherently ascetic, a stripping away of the non-essential, an enforced abstinence from sensual pleasure.

We can only know peace through our bodies. See also: pain.

Some lobotomy patients report feeling pain but not being bothered by it.

One morning, during isolation, I have the urge to pirouette in my slippers on the polished wood. Fuck it, I want to move. Some sense fails and I hit the floor. My spine judders like an old gate. I'm not injured, but I am aware of a limitation, a new boundary of self, which is itself an injury.

'Pain has an element of blank,' says Emily Dickinson, but it is not blank enough.

Or perhaps it is too blank and that is why I'm writing about it.

It started as if. As if a bee had stung me. As if hot wires were being threaded through my body. Now it is its own thing. It has driven off comparison, metaphor, any allies in language.

There can be no history of peace. Peace is now or not at all.

Notes

The epigraph is taken from American artist and writer David Wojnarowicz's journal entry on 20 May 1979 (David Wojnarowicz Papers, Fales Library and Special Collections, New York University Libraries, MSS 092, Series 1, Box 1, Folder 10).

'The Crew of the *Zeewijk*, 1727': In December 1727, the crew of the *Zeewijk* marooned two young sailors on separate deserted islands off the coast of what is now called Western Australia as punishment for 'the gruesome sin of Sodom and Gomorrah' (van de Graef, A. (2014). *The Journal by Adriaen van der Graef, Under-steersman Aboard the Ship Zeewijk. 1726–1728*. Translated by A. De Jong. Fremantle, Australia: Western Australian Maritime Museum).

'Caravaggisti' is the name given to artists influenced by Michelangelo Merisi da Caravaggio. As part of their ongoing feud, Giovanni Baglione painted a second version of *Sacred Love and Profane Love* in which he depicted Caravaggio as a sodomitical devil.

'Travelling Companion': American artists Paul Cadmus and Jared French travelled together through Europe in the early 1930s.

'Pool Sweet, 2019': Peter Schlesinger, David Hockney's then-lover and the model for *Peter Getting out of Nick's Pool* (1966), posed against the hood of a car, not in a pool.

'Two Figures': Francis Bacon's *Two Figures* (1953) depicts Bacon and his lover Peter Lacy locked in a sadomasochistic embrace.

'Landscape near Malabata': Bacon's *Landscape near Malabata, Tangier* (1963) depicts the place where Lacy was buried following his death, aged forty-six, in 1962.

'Unfinished Portrait of Two Figures': George Dyer, another of Bacon's lovers, was found dead, aged thirty-seven, on the eve of Bacon's retrospective at the Grand Palais, Paris, in 1971.

'She sent him a handwritten note: *I'm sure you remember me. My fans would feel cheated if they didn't see how I look in my hospital bed*' adapts part of its title from a letter actor Candy Darling wrote to photographer Peter Hujar.

'Loving Cup': Vivian Forbes took his own life following the death of his lover, British painter Glyn Philpot, in 1937. Philpot painted this portrait of Forbes in 1915, the year they met.

'Pas de Deux for Silhouette and Swan': Against tradition, the swans in Matthew Bourne's *Swan Lake* (1995) are danced by men. In Act II, the Prince intends to drown himself in a public park until he meets the Swan and they dance a pas de deux. The ballet's composer, Pyotr Ilyich Tchaikovsky, had many romantic and sexual relationships with men before his sudden death, aged fifty-three, in 1893.

'Fragments on the Myth of Cy Twombly': American artists Cy Twombly and Robert Rauschenberg, like Achilles and

Patroclus, were in love. This poem also responds in part to Robert Rauschenberg's series of photographs *Cy + Roman Steps (I–V)* (1952).

'the house i will be born in': *stamvader* is Dutch for ancestor; literally: tribe father.

'School Dictionary': Heartsease is another name for wild pansy.

'Homebirth' was written after Bushwig Festival of Drag, Music & Love 2018 where I saw Lady Quesa'Dilla launch the house of JEM, which she named after Cuban American Queer academic José Esteban Muñoz.

'Peace Body Pain Body': The quote from Emily Dickinson is taken from *The Poems of Emily Dickinson: Reading Edition*, edited by Ralph W. Franklin, Cambridge, Mass.: The Belknap Press of Harvard University Press, Copyright © 1998, 1999 by the President and Fellows of Harvard College. Copyright © 1951, 1955 by the President and Fellows of Harvard College. Copyright © renewed 1979, 1983 by the President and Fellows of Harvard College. Copyright © 1914, 1918, 1919, 1924, 1929, 1930, 1932, 1935, 1937, 1942 by Martha Dickinson Bianchi. Copyright © 1952, 1957, 1958, 1963, 1965 by Mary L. Hampson. Used by permission. All rights reserved.

*

Acknowledgements

This book was written on the unceded lands of the Turrbal and Jagera peoples. I acknowledge and pay my respects to their Elders past and present.

I'm grateful to the editors and staff of the following publications where a number of these poems first appeared, some in earlier versions: *Australian Poetry Anthology*, *Australian Poetry Journal*, *Best of Australian Poems 2022*, *Cordite Poetry Review*, *HEAT*, *Impossible Archetype*, *Island*, *Meanjin Quarterly*, *Overland*, *Peril Magazine*, *Rabbit*, *TEXT*, *The Tundish Review* and *Westerly Magazine*.

I'm grateful to the writers who guided and supported me as I wrote these poems: Torrey Atkin, Mindy Gill, Sarah Holland-Batt, Ella Jeffery, Rebecca Jessen, Felicity Plunkett, Alex Philp, the QUT poets and Rohan Wilson.

Special thanks to Sarah for being the kind of poet I aspire to be, to Mindy and Alex for being angels, and to Bec for always meeting me in the usual spot.

Thank you to Queensland Poetry, Arts Queensland, and the Arts Queensland Thomas Shapcott Poetry Prize 2022 judges Maria Takolander and Stuart Barnes.

Thank you to Queensland Poetry, Arts Queensland, and the Val Vallis Award 2023 judges Zenobia Frost and Benjamin Dodds for recognising 'Fragments on the Myth of Cy Twombly'.

Thank you also to Maria Takolander for a generous and incisive edit.

Thank you to UQP, especially Aviva Tuffield and Felicity Dunning for your encouragement and expertise.

Finally, this wouldn't be the book it is without my first and best reader, my sweet love, Torrey—thank you.

Milton Keynes UK
Ingram Content Group UK Ltd.
UKHW022343020823
426203UK00017B/739

9 780702 266263